EMERGE

Blessings & Rituals

for Unsheltering

from the
STILLSPEAKING WRITERS' GROUP

The Stillspeaking Writers' Group is composed of United Church of Christ ministers and writers who collaborate on resources for people in the church, outside the church, and not sure about the church.

© 2020 United Church of Christ

Local Churches, Conferences, Associations, and other settings of the United Church of Christ may use these reflections for any not-for-profit use by any medium (including by not limited to print and website), so long as credit is given to the reflection's author and to this resource. The reflections must be used in their entirety and the content may not be altered in any way. For other uses and permissions questions, contact the United Church of Christ National Setting through the permissions team of The Pilgrim Press (permission@thepilgrimpress.com).

Contents

Invocation • Blessings and Rituals for Gathering
Prayer for the First Time Leaving Shelter 6
Blessing for Returning to Joyous Spaces 7
Ritual of Welcome for Virtual Worship 9
Blessing for the Still-Empty Pews 11
Blessing for the Reunion of Old and Young 12
Ritual for Returning to the Office 13
Prayer When Feeling Apprehensive about Grocery Shopping 14
Prayer for Returning to the Church Building (Maybe) 15
Litany for Passing the Peace 16

Hymn of Praise
Blessing for Bats 20

Confession • Blessings and Rituals for Unburdening
Prayer for Worship Leaders Wondering If People Will Come Back 24
Meditation for When People Who Ignore
   Safety Recommendations Are Making You Mad as Heck 26
Prayer of Impotence 27
Prayer to Release Doom Scrolling 28
Prayer from Someone Who Already Knew Scarcity 30
Blessing for Mother Earth as Pollution Increases 32
Confession of Those Who Bought Too Much 33
Prayer for Needing Touch 34
Ritual for Breathing in the Breath of God 35

Hymn of Thanksgiving
Jigsaw Puzzle Antiphon 38

Proclamation of Good News

Creed for the Marginalized 42

Litany of Purpose 43

Intercession ◆ Blessings and Rituals for Healing

Curse on Covid-19 46

Prayer for U.S.-China Relations 48

Lament for Flunking Racism, Again 49

Blessing for Mixed Feelings 50

Prayer on the Edge of the Inside 52

Blessing for a Face Mask 53

Prayer for Pentecostal Wind 54

Ritual During My Anxiety Attack 55

Prayer for Self-Love and Social Justice 57

Hymn of Faith

Hymn for Waiting in Faith: When Noah Sent a Dove to Fly 60

Communion ◆ Blessings and Rituals for Remembering

Prayer of Great Thanksgiving 64

Ritual for Authentic Participation 67

Litany of Farewell to Google Classroom 68

Prayer for Steadfast Supporters and New Economics 70

Litany for When We Start to Forget 72

Prayer for the Pooch That Is Suddenly Alone
and Doesn't Understand Why 74

Prayer When Missing the Quarantine 76

Prayer If the Virus Lasts Longer than I Think I Can 78

Blessing for the Future 79

Benediction

Litany of Sending and Blessing 82

Contributors 84

INVOCATION

♦

BLESSINGS & RITUALS FOR GATHERING

Prayer for the First Time Leaving Shelter

Now I walk me out my door.
I pray thee, Lord, protect from spores.
Bless, dear Lord, the care I take
not to worsen this outbreak.
Guide me safely through the day
and bring me home, masked and OK.
Amen.

—**QUINN G. CALDWELL**

Blessing for Returning to Joyous Spaces

Bless the dance floors and the...
coffee shops,
patios,
karaoke stages,
arenas,
bowling alleys,
barbershops and salons,
gyms,
bars and wineries,
arcades,
theaters,
malls and markets,
art galleries,
amusement parks,
and, and, and...

Bless our grieving hearts
as we mourn the places we've loved
that won't reopen.

Bless our restless hearts
as we resist the temptation
to gather before it's safe.

Blessings and Rituals for Unsheltering | EMERGE

Bless our restless hearts
as we resist the temptation
to gather before it's safe.

Bless our fearful hearts
as service workers among us
provide joy at the risk of exposure.

Bless our grateful hearts
as we cling to
the sounds and smells,
the colors and textures,
and the sacred memories
of the places we love –
as we gather again.

—MARCHAÉ GRAIR

Ritual of Welcome for Virtual Worship

God is good! *All the time!* Welcome to the Church in Diaspora on this Blessed Blursday, Xth day of the Zth month of the year of Coronavirus 2020! But who's counting?

Welcome if you're watching in hi-def, lo-fi or have to keep rebooting your screen or your soul because it's so worn out. When glitches and hiccups happen, remember God dwells in the interruptions, too.

Welcome to you if you are old or young, or a little bit of each; queer or straight, or a little bit of each; doubting or believing, saint or sinner, or a little bit of each. Welcome to people of all colors, all genders, all body shapes and sizes, all physical, mental and emotional abilities and moments. Because we are here and there and everywhere, yet somehow still together as One today, this Body of Christ is whole and a little more perfect.

Now remember you *have* a whole body even though it sometimes seems—staring into screens—that you are nothing but eyes and brains. Welcome all of yourself to this moment, with a hand on your heart, and one on your belly, breathing more deeply, remembering that in many languages 'breath' and 'spirit' are the same word.

Now reach out your blessing hands in every direction. Welcome the creatures you are sharing space with, then your neighbors, then strangers afar to this moment of peace and worship. Send out peace with your body, and feel it echo back.

Peace be with you!

—**MOLLY BASKETTE**

Blessing for the Still-Empty Pews

The front row used to get teased
by the other rows: "No one sits there!" But no more.
Never have they *all* felt so neglected, so lonely.
Now there is only the occasional spider. But,

Spiders don't sit, linger, listen, and lounge.
Spiders don't have children who kick and fidget.
Spiders don't make seats creak with delight.
Their hearts aren't quickened by meeting the Great
  Carpenter.

Blessed are the church pews, chairs, and benches
welcoming butts, backs, thighs of every shape and size
without judgment, without complaint, without any
  preferences
yet still beaming to be claimed as someone's regular,
  favorite spot!

Blessed are all these mercy seats
that wait for us
but not
alone.

—MATT LANEY

Blessing for the Reunion of Old and Young

Bless the sliding of this window,
the opening of this door.

Speed these feet,
the tiny and the large.

Hallow the hollow between these two arms,
filled again finally by a small, warm body.

Consecrate this meeting:
smooth cheeks and wrinkled,
spotted hands and clear,
bone of bone,
flesh rejoined to flesh.

Bless, Holy Spirit,
these fast-flowing waters.
Amen.

—**QUINN G. CALDWELL**

Ritual for Returning to the Office

Dust spiritually
Dust physically

Wipe spiritually
Wipe physically

Disinfect
Repeat

Open windows and vinyl blinds
Open windows in the heart

Give thanks for the work
Throw out what is not useful anymore

Go back to work
Go forward to prayer

—DONNA SCHAPER

Prayer When Feeling Apprehensive about Grocery Shopping

I'm going to buy groceries now, God.
I'm wearing a mask. I have sanitizer.
There'll be glass between me and the cashier.
I'll be in and out in 20 minutes.
I'll wash my hands the second I get home.
Everything will be fine.
Won't it?
Breathe.
Do you get this, dear God? That I'm nervous?
Grocery shopping used to be a chore, not a risk.
Tell me I'm not being ridiculous.
Don't say, "Get over yourself."
Don't say anything.
Just take my hand.
(Is it safe to hold hands with you?)
Just come with me, up and down the aisles.
If you come, I'll be fine.
You are the Lord of the bread aisle, the soup cans,
and the frozen peas.
You push my cart.
You comfort me.

—MARY LUTI

Prayer for Returning to the Church Building (Maybe)

God, I miss that place, the praise, those people,
candles, bread and cup, the doors, the steeple.

But honestly God, I'm uncertain about going back.
Must we pass the peace? Will others wear a mask?

Will we sing ourselves sick? Always in long sleeves and pants?
Can I be spiritual while thinking about disinfectants?

God, you said in every shadowy valley, there you would be
so I'm trusting in your rod and your staff to protect me.

May my (individual and sanitized) cup overflow;
may goodness and mercy follow wherever I go.

Even into your house.

—MATT LANEY

Litany for Passing the Peace

We cannot touch just now,
not yet.

We cannot shake, embrace, slap each other on the back,
or kiss,
not yet.

We cannot move around the space,
up and down the aisles,
jostle each other,
trip over kids,
reach down the pew to greet
the elderly gent who can't get up,
scan for the couple who came last week,
hope this raucous time will go on and on—
or pray that it won't, and the organist will cut it off
with the intro to the next hymn—we can't,
not yet.

But the peace that passes understanding
is not like a virus.
It doesn't need contact to infect.
It's like the Spirit and the wind:
it goes wherever it wills,
wherever we send it.

Through webs and nets and wires,
it googles and zooms to everyone
whose heart needs peace,
and to every place
there is no peace.
And we will share it now:
the peace of Christ be with you!
And also with you!

—**MARY LUTI**

HYMN OF PRAISE

Blessing for Bats

Only scientists
could love
rodents with
pterodactyl wings
and fangs,
that cling to
creepy places;
docs who
poke and prod,
swab and smear,
tickle and tag
when all bats want
is to flap about
under the stars,
feast on mosquitos,
make babies,
hang with their friends,
echolocating,
winging it
and loving it.

Blessed are you, *Chiroptera*!
Be as batty as our Creator
made you to be!
The truth is we envy you—
not just the flying,
but your resilience
to pathogens,
including the pathogen
of humanity.

—MATT LANEY

CONFESSION

◆

BLESSINGS & RITUALS
FOR UNBURDENING

Prayer for Worship Leaders Wondering If People Will Come Back

Great Maker,

We've adapted, pivoted, leapfrogged our way to virtual church. We're down to under 10 glitches a Sunday. People love it! And I do too. Those old couples cuddled and peering into the screen. Those Zoombombing 6-year-olds making silly faces!

There is gift in this Brave New Church. In some ways we are closer to each other, closer to you, and more creative as a people. Yet still I fear the cursed cursor, the tech tribulations, the pixelated watchers. (How can people be so late even to online church?)

I dance faster and brainstorm better and edit longer, trying to make all things new every week so they don't get bored. What if they wander off after a more fetching online community? What if they forget their longing to be bodies in space together—the beauty and power of the Christ "en carne"? What if, when all this is over, they are still afraid to come back?

What if this is it?

Remind me again that wherever two or more are gathered in your name, you are there among us. You make the faith new in every generation, and you are not done with us yet. Remind me, when I go overboard with new product development that there is power, too, in repetition and familiarity.

Great Maker, you rested on the seventh day, and I can too.

—MOLLY BASKETTE

Meditation for When People Who Ignore Safety Recommendations Are Making You Mad as Heck

Jesus, you said pray for your enemies.
There's sneaky wisdom in that.
If you're really praying for someone
it's a lot harder to hate them,
and if you keep it up sincerely over time
you might even start to love them.
What happens after that is anybody's guess.
My guess, good Jesus,
is that it all leads to meeting you in them
and to discovering that they are wounded, too.
What happens then, once I know that?
Once I learn we share one single shattered heart?
I've never been there, Jesus, I don't know.
But as the heat rises in my brain,
the censure, consternation, and the rage, I wish I did.
Because right now I just want to haul off and pummel them,
smack some sense into them, smack them good.
Teach me to pray.

—MARY LUTI

Prayer of Impotence

How do I pray when my job is gone, God? How do I pray when I can't go out, can't find a test, have a pain in my chest or side, and no one cares? What kind of prayer is desperation? Do you hear? Do you show up in the unemployment check? And if not? Then what? Up a creek, that's me, without a paddle.

—**DONNA SCHAPER**

Prayer to Release Doom Scrolling

Aliens have taken over my brain, Lord. I can't stop reading FaceTwitChatNews.™ My bones melt with fear within me, my heart goes numb, my eyes bleed from late night viewing without blue-light-blocking glasses.

Surely the next meme, gif, rant, or think piece will satisfy my soul's hunger for meaning and hope. Without a doubt, if I attend longer to what my "friends" are sharing, I will feel deeply sated, instead of the compare-and-despair I usually feel after too much gorging on the socials.
Don't you always tell us to Share and Like, Lord?

No, you say? Not like that? It's time to turn off the device? Like, all the way off? Not just put it to sleep, nor stumble around the bedroom in the dark looking for the charger so I can be assured that when morning comes my phone and I can pick up where we left off? But what if I miss the late-breaking truth that will finally set me free?

Yes, Lord, I hear you above this noise. It is hard to let go of this solid little rectangle that promises so much and delivers so little in the way of peace and insight. I can do it if you just reach for my other hand. Now. Thank you.

Hold me while I fall asleep. Amen.

—MOLLY BASKETTE

Prayer from Someone Who Already Knew Scarcity

Dear God:

I'm pissed off.
The bills were already late.
The collectors were already calling.
The shifts were already too long.
The shifts already disappeared.
The appointments were already postponed.
The house already needed work.
The family already needed new clothes.
The food was already too expensive.
It was already exhausting just to live.

And now this.
Now the hoarding and the panic
from those who perform scarcity
because they've never actually known it.

Now the discarding of my life
because the health care
I already couldn't afford
is now even more beyond my reach.

Now, in a downturned economy,
companies get bailouts
yet I can't get enough help.
Where do I place this anger?

Where are you, God, in this moment?
I am pissed,
and I'm tired of asking "How long, O Lord?"
Can you just answer the question?

Writer's note: I encourage reading this prayer and if possible, finding a safe space to scream. Rinse and repeat. God can take it.

—MARCHAÉ GRAIR

Blessing for Mother Earth as Pollution Increases

You sent us all to our rooms for bad behavior
to think about all that we had done and had left undone
while you put your feet up, read some romance and just
 took a breather.
Soon we felt the pinch, decided it was no fun, and that we
 were done.

Hope you enjoyed your extended Mother's Day!
But the market is down, people need work, and the kids are
 bonkers.
We are warriors now, defending our normal,
even though that was killing us too.

Bless you Gaia, Great Mother, Eco-Sister, Auntie Terra!
Bless us too, because though we fail to honor it, we are you.
Bless lungs and trees, breathing together.
Bless flesh and soil, earthy wrappers both.
Bless veins and rivers, running as one.
Bless bones and stones, like unto like.

Bless us with compassion for our Great Matriarch
as her cough, infection, and fever returns.

—MATT LANEY

Confession of Those Who Bought Too Much

You promised living water;
I built a dam.

You were preparing a table for me;
I prepared my own.

You emptied yourself;
I filled my basement.

Bless by your Holy Spirit, O God,
this unrighteous pile,
fruit of a fearful heart pretending to practicality.

Harrow now this basement
and transform this hoard.

Make it source and beginning of my generosity:
broken and shared, poured out for many,
flowing and free, for the forgiveness of this sin.

O God, transform this stockpile
into the thing that transforms me. Amen.

—QUINN G. CALDWELL

Blessings and Rituals for Unsheltering | EMERGE

Prayer for Needing Touch

It's been 73 days since my last hug, Great Heart. I felt my whole body go electric when the checkout clerk accidentally brushed my hand giving me a receipt last Tuesday.

I have a whole family at home I can hug, Holy One, but I'm greedy and I want more. I am a seed that wants to be sown across many fields, cross-pollinating my care into community.

I don't know what I will do if church doesn't re-open for a year or more, Lord. Those eight handshakes during the passing of the peace were the only touch I got all week during normal times. It was hard enough to live on such short rations. And now I'm dying of skin hunger.

Jesus, you are God with skin on. You gave yourself a body so you could touch and be touched. Find me a person, a stable pod, a cohort of huggers until we find a cure, so I can be like you, reaching out to heal myself and others, letting them touch my wounds, gently reveal my realness, remind myself that I'm alive.

In the meantime, I will touch myself.

—**MOLLY BASKETTE**

Ritual for Breathing in the Breath of God

Breathe in deeply and hold while praying:
You have given us new meaning, O God, in the words "shortness of breath."

Breathe out forcefully and stretch while praying:
Holy Spirit, draw near and relieve me of my hammers, my nails, my thorns, my self-punishments, my judgment of others.

Breathe in deeply and hold while praying:
Breathe a new breath in me, let it be fresher than mouthwash, more amusing than amazing.

Breathe out forcefully and stretch while praying:
Take away from my shortness in spirit and add unconditional spaciousness. Let me breathe easier, spiritually and physically.

—DONNA SCHAPER

HYMN OF THANKSGIVING

Jigsaw Puzzle Antiphon

O, thou passer of hours!
O, thou strange beguiler!
O, thou dumbest of activities!
O jigsaw puzzle!

O frustration of assembly, pray for us.
O brief sense of triumph, pray for us.
O temptation to glue, pray for us.
O gloom of dismemberment, pray for us.

O lost piece, have mercy on us.
O incorrect fit, have mercy on us.
O cat on the table, have mercy on us.

O, thou jigsaw puzzle!

When we could not think,
you gave us mindlessness.

When nothing would resolve,
you made order from madness.

When we did not know what to do,
you gave us a purpose, slight and safe.

O, jigsaw puzzle!
O thou Mostly Useless,
O thou Bad Metaphor
O thou Least Fun,
raised for a time to high estate,
now sunk back to obscurity:
You were a small pleasure when pleasure was rare.

O jigsaw puzzle,
bless you.
Amen.

—**QUINN G. CALDWELL**

PROCLAMATION
OF GOOD NEWS

Creed for the Marginalized

I am powerful
I deserve to live
Joy is my birthright

I am beautiful
I deserve to thrive
Community is my anchor

I am worthy
I deserve to be free
Liberation is my legacy

You can't take what my ancestors taught me
You can't destroy what my ancestors created
You can't heal in me what was never broken

You don't have to honor me for my life to matter
You don't have to save me because I'm saving myself
You don't have to notice me for this miracle to keep unfolding

I am the miracle
Because I live
And believe I deserve to

—MARCHAÉ GRAIR

Litany of Purpose

How to find purpose in times like these?

Especially since we don't know the name of the times or what the old name for the old times really was or what the new name for the new times will really be.

What story will we tell about ourselves during the pandemic?

I was fine.
I survived.
I coped.

Or:
I called myself beloved, and the earth called my name back to me.

—DONNA SCHAPER

INTERCESSION

◆

BLESSINGS & RITUALS FOR HEALING

Curse on Covid-19

Maker of the Universe,
You want us to respect and care for all creatures,
not curse and destroy them.
But couldn't we make an exception for this virus?
It's terrible, and doing so much harm.
You yourself were not above cursing things.
Remember how unhappy you once were with us?
You sent a flood.
And Jesus didn't go easy on the fig tree.
He cursed it, and it withered, just like that.
I don't understand why.
But I do know this:
Cursing shouldn't be done lightly or often,
but now seems like a perfect time.
People have suffered so much.
So, forgive me if I'm crossing any lines here,
but here goes:

You malevolent horrible virus,
you microscopic nasty,
you pox with spikey crown:
I maledict and curse you!
I imprecate and revile you!
I execrate and scorn you!
I summon science to annihilate you,
to bleach you and to wipe you,
to test you and to trace you,
to send you writhing into the void!
With righteous strength I oppose you!
In the name of Life, I damn you:
Be damned, and be gone!
Be damned, and be gone!
Be damned, and be gone!

—MARY LUTI

Prayer for U.S.–China Relations

Dear Lord, the relationship between China and the U.S. has been strained for quite some time now, and the Covid-19 crisis has turned up the heat.

Lord, there are many who know the pointed sting of being scapegoated and stigmatized for mass tragedies. The hurt inflicted by racial and ethnic prejudice cause psychological scars that last for generations.

So today, as we pray for healing from the Coronavirus, we also pray for healing in our international relations. May the economic interdependence between our nation and China re-emphasize the need for diplomacy. And may the rewards of that interdependence secure livable wages and adequate health care for the masses of laborers in both countries.

Crown leaders with your wisdom. Deliver us from unexamined nationalism. Show us how much we need each other. And let this virus have no victory, as we find in it our common humanity and as we come away from it with a greater commitment to build your kin-dom globally.

In the name of the Christ who makes us one we pray. Amen.

—**KENNETH L. SAMUEL**

Lament for Flunking Racism, Again

The white people in our congregation knew very few people who died from the virus. The black people in our congregation attended multiple zoom funerals per week.

New York City is the kind of place that thinks of itself—rightly, arrogantly—as an epicenter. And what a racist epicenter: more transit workers died than first responders in the first months of pandemic, a majority black workforce.

We are flunking, again.

—DONNA SCHAPER

Blessing for Mixed Feelings

God, they say feelings are a package deal. The yuck and the yum come bundled.

God, they say that all feelings are from you—it's what we do with them that matters.

But what do we do when our feelings come not tidily trussed but messily tangled, like a fine silver chain that won't be undone no matter how long we labor over it? It sits in a box waiting for a miracle-worker.

I take them out again, the pile of feelings. And this time, I ask you to bless them before I begin the work:

Bless the anger and the irritation. Bless the gratitude and the joy-sparks. Bless the compassion and the selfishness, the fear and the courage, the gloom and the hope, the listlessness and the purposeful action. Bless the love in my life, and bless the distance—emotional and physical—between those I would reune with. Bless the stress, and bless the serenity.

Bless it all, the whole mess, and remind me that having a rainbow of feelings is your light, prismed into spectrum.

I feel a little more ease now. I can see where to begin, to gently untangle, pull there, push there, rest there…and find how it all fits together in one unbroken, beautiful strand.

—**MOLLY BASKETTE**

Prayer on the Edge of the Inside

Richard Rohr says that we are often on the edge of the inside. What kind of place is that for someone who feels like an outsider but is really an insider? Who feels like an outsider in a time when so many feel way too scared to go outside? What happens to a world where everybody is afraid of everybody else but doesn't want to stay inside? Is that a world where everything is an edge or on edge?

—**DONNA SCHAPER**

Blessing for a Face Mask

God of health and wholeness,
of neighbor love and kindness,
bless this mask, my slight shield
against great ills:

Bless the fabric that repels the drops,
the ties that go behind my ears,
the wire that fits snug against my nose,
the folds that cup my chin.

Make me grateful for my mask
even when it makes me hot,
even when I look funny in it,
even when I'm dying to take it off.

Bless me also, and everyone
who for their own and others' sakes
put on this holy inconvenience every day,
our minds made up to love.

—**MARY LUTI**

Prayer for Pentecostal Wind

Blow a new wind into our lungs, ventilate us, let us breathe all the way to freedom, by the power of your holiest and most whole Spirit. And make us allies of those who can't breathe, whose breath is halted, whose pace is slow, who have been too hurt for too long to go on. As we remember the people who died alone, as we remember the nurses sitting alone on the stairs wondering what to do next, as we remember the doctors who could do nothing to reestablish breath, let us point to the fresh wind—the freedom wind—of Pentecost, and new ways for new days. Amen.

—**DONNA SCHAPER**

Ritual During My Anxiety Attack

When my skin keeps crawling,
wrap me in your loving embrace.
When my breath keeps quickening,
Give me sweet release.

Pause to bless something you hear, smell, see, touch, or taste.

When my weeping consumes my being,
lead me toward self-compassion.
When the "what ifs" feel too scary,
help me stay present in your presence.

Pause to bless something you hear, smell, see, touch, or taste.

Tend to the undercurrents of emotions
that burst forward in ways beyond my control,
and release me from any grief and shame
I carry just for feeling my feelings.

Pause to bless something you hear, smell, see, touch, or taste.

Ground me in my divine resilience:
I am still here, I am still worthy.
Ground me in your divine companionship:
you are still here, I am never alone.

Repeat the final stanza as many times as needed.

Writer's note: Engaging the five senses during an anxiety attack can lessen the symptoms and length of the attack.

—MARCHAÉ GRAIR

Prayer for Self-Love and Social Justice

Great Flow of Justice, even larger than great waters, dividing and reuniting, place us in that gymnastic zone, the judgment-free place, where our fat and our flaws matter less than our faith, our lollygagging and loneliness matter less than our love, and our own judgments and jealousies matter less than your justice.

Let this virus be the catalyst for real change in ourselves, each other, and our beloved country. Let it teach us how one life flows into another, always and regularly. Amen.

—DONNA SCHAPER

HYMN OF FAITH

Hymn for Waiting in Faith: When Noah Sent a Dove to Fly

When Noah sent a dove to fly
across the ebbing sea
to seek a sign of life's return,
he waited patiently.

Not knowing if she'd find a thing,
he waited patiently,
and prayed the dove along her way
toward unknown mystery.

And as she winged her way on prayer
toward unknown mystery,
already you had freed the land
and planted olive trees.

Already, as she circled high,
you'd planted olive trees,
already made the branch she'd take,
its green and silver leaves:

Already made new earth a jewel
of green and silver leaves,
while Noah still in patience prayed,
still scanned the cloud and breeze.

Our patient prayers are like the dove
that scans through clouds and breeze
for signs that in foreseeing love
you're planting olive trees.

We hope she'll bring a branch, but more,
we ask for faith to know
that while we're praying unaware,
the trees you're planting grow.

Tunes: Land of Rest, Dundee
CM 8.6.8.6

—MARY LUTI

COMMUNION

♦

BLESSINGS & RITUALS
FOR REMEMBERING

Prayer of Great Thanksgiving

God of life and all creatures,
from the first day to this day
you have showered us with gifts
of mercy and grace.

From the first day to this day
you have sent us signs and wonders,
prophets and dreamers
to call us to yourself,
and offer us your grace:

healing for our brokenness,
release from our pain,
calm for mental stress,
peace for soul-grief and regret,
pardon to remedy our sin
and justice to make life whole and glad.

Thanks and praise to you for all your gifts,
and most of all for Jesus,
our wounded risen brother and friend.
He abides with us here in mystery,
as he abided that last night among his friends.

From his safe and holy hands
you give us this, our daily bread,
his body surrendered for us.

From his safe and holy hands
we also now receive
this brimming cup,
this life poured out for us.

We remember him now,
as he told us to do,
whenever we break his bread
and drink his cup at our tables.

As we take him to ourselves
in this time of illness and fear,
we remember before you
the people we love,
the enemies we do not love,
and all who suffer in this world,
the frail and falling sparrows
on whom your eye is fixed.

Blessings and Rituals for Unsheltering | **EMERGE**

By the grace and power of the Spirit
let all who share this bread and cup
be one in Christ,
no matter where we are,
near or far, together or apart:
one in heart and purpose,
one in love and service.
one in fearless witness
to new heavens and new earth:
that joyous realm to come
where, by your promise,
there will be no sickness and dying,
no tears and grieving,
but only joy, only life, only justice,
only you.

All praise and thanks to you,
God of all life, now and forever.
Amen.

—**MARY LUTI**

Ritual for Authentic Participation

Mute. Unmute.

Unmute me, O God, and remind me to say what I think and feel.

Mute. Unmute.

Let me say what I need to say without anger or accusation or judgment.

Mute. Unmute.

Let me test and consider if being unmuted is helpful. Amen.

—**DONNA SCHAPER**

Litany of Farewell to Google Classroom

Leader: In March of 2020, the _____ family called Google Classroom to be its primary educator.

Google Classroom: You have seven assignments due this Friday.

Family: We thank you for your time among us, for getting us through. We forgive you for all the ways you hurt us. We ask your forgiveness for never checking your to-do list. Your influence on us will not leave us when we log out of you, hopefully forever.

Leader: Do you, the members of the _____ family, release Google Classroom from the duties of primary educator?

Family: Oh dear Lord, yes.

Google Classroom: Mr. West has posted a new assignment.

Leader: Do you offer your encouragement for Google Classroom to serve as educator to others?

Family: I mean, I guess. It was good to have when we needed it, but it was, like, really hard for a while there.

Leader: Let us pray.

All: O God,
we give thanks for tech that gets us through emergencies.
Thank you, too, for teaching us how important
flesh and blood, brick and mortar are.
Bless our return to desks and classrooms
bodies and boards,
conversation without lag,
touch without screens.
Return this technology to its proper role:
helpmeet and support.
Receive now this better-than-nothing offering,
the mixed fruit of these last months—
frustration and learning
fear and growth
so, so much clicking.
Hold them in grace,
and guide us back to the embodied world in safety.

*Google Classroom: You have 7,349 missing assignments.
Selah.*

—**QUINN G. CALDWELL**

Prayer for Steadfast Supporters and New Economics

Gracious God,

We open the doors of our church building again with gratitude for those whose financial support has sustained us through this crisis. We thank you, God, for those who gave to support the church even when they could not come to the building. We thank you for those who gave to support the church even when their own finances were in jeopardy. We thank you for those who gave to support the church even when the U.S. economy was in sharp decline because of the Covid-19 quarantine.

Lord, we are grateful that the steadfast stewardship of your people has seen us through what we pray has been the worst of this Coronavirus financial calamity. Help us now to be attentive to those who could not financially support the church because of job loss or drastic reductions of income. Use us now to show them how much they are valued in your family of faith.

And, Lord, prepare all of us as we step into a new economy. We don't know all that those transitions will bring, but we are confident that your grace will prove to be sufficient—as it has been, as it is now, as it will be forever. Amen.

—KENNETH L. SAMUEL

Litany for When We Start to Forget

In God's presence
I remember you

I remember you
Old people dead in nursing homes and solitary apartments
I remember you
Middle-aged men with underlying conditions, working one day, dead the next
I remember you
Little ones dead of strange syndromes
I remember you
Black people and brown people dead in unthinkable numbers
I remember you
Nurses and orderlies, doctors and EMTs, dead for serving and tending
I remember you
Cleaners and meat packers, bus drivers, cashiers, and delivery people dead because you were just working—you had to work
I remember you

Prisoners, migrants, and people living on the streets dead for not having any say in it
I remember you
Parents dead, siblings dead, cousins dead, friends dead, spouses dead, grandparents dead, neighbors dead, famous people dead, not famous people dead
I remember you
People I know, my own dear dead
I remember you
With reverence and lament
I remember you
In hope and love
I remember you all

In God's presence
I remember you
Amen.

—**MARY LUTI**

Prayer for the Pooch That Is Suddenly Alone and Doesn't Understand Why

For a time, a full staff of warm hands and laps,
an endless buffet of tasty crumbs and scraps!
Walks and walks and walks again,
and not one trip to the groomer's den!

Now, suddenly, he's in the pen a lot more,
tail drooping, sad puppy eyes fixed on the door.
Lover of creatures great and small,
bless our pets, one and all:

The fish with a less steady diet.
The gerbil, grateful for more quiet.
The cat, free-ranging the house like a badass.
The reptile pondering the mystery of glass.

And this pack animal, shut into a crate,
who doesn't get the sudden need to wait.
these pent-up pups now spend most of their day,
wondering how to make humans sit and stay.

Oh G-O-D who knows D-O-G so well,
comfort them in this moment of canine-hell.
Let them feel your fingers scratching behind soft ears.
Be the steady lap that removes all their worst fears.

—**MATT LANEY**

Prayer When Missing the Quarantine

God, it may sound strange,
but sometimes I miss the quarantine.
I miss making bread,
doing puzzles,
helping the kids with math,
watching the cats do cat things,
not getting dressed,
giving my family bad haircuts,
singing with my friends on Zoom.

It wasn't all sweetness and light.
You know it, Lord.
Some days were a misery.
I'm not romanticizing,
I'm just confessing there are things I miss.
It's the new normal now,
and we might not do those things again.
At least not that way.
I'm sad about that.

Be tender with me, God.
And in good time,
refine my sadness into thanks,
so that when I start to miss a moment from those days,
my heart will lighten, lift to you, and say:
Oh, what a gift that was, dear Lord!
How good you were to me!
How good you always are to me!

—MARY LUTI

Prayer If the Virus Lasts Longer than I Think I Can

I don't know where I am going today and tomorrow; I just know my lust and my desire for more of what I had yesterday. I also know that I am your child and beloved. I am not forgotten by you.

Send me one sign today that I am still and all beloved. Just one. And when I know I am beloved, let me get back on track—whatever track might be. Amen.

—DONNA SCHAPER

Blessing for the Future

Bless, O God,
the unanswerable
the hypothetical
the possible

Bless the silence
the shrug
the hard to say
the "who knows?"
the "have to wait and see"

Bless the markers
the absence of markers
the path
the no path
the indistinct
the clearing

Bless the arriving life
the nothing-normal-about-it new normal
the un-scouted
the future
the unknown

Bless you in it
the presence
the firm
the knowing
the power
the same love

Bless you in it
the center
the serene
the hidden near
the gleaming
the boundless mercy
the same love

The same love
Here and there

The same love
Now and when

—MARY LUTI

BENEDICTION

Litany of Sending and Blessing

Our worship has ended,
but its gifts remain:

Tuck its praise inside you.
Take its goodness with you.

Drink from its wells of lasting peace.
Live by its light, its courage and grace,
and don't be afraid.

Seek to serve.
In plenty or want,
find ways to share.

Discern the truth and tell it,
resist all wrong,
and don't be afraid.

Regard all people as your people.

In hard times and good
take care of yourself,
take care of your people,
and don't be afraid.

And may the blessing of God, our life,
the friendship of Christ, our healer,
and the daring of the Spirit, our truth,
be ours today, and every day to come.
Amen.

—MARY LUTI

Contributors

Molly Baskette is Senior Minister of the First Church of Berkeley, California. Her newest book is *Bless This Mess: A Modern Guide to Faith and Parenting in a Chaotic World.*

Quinn G. Caldwell is a father, husband, homesteader, and preacher living in rural upstate New York. He is the author of *All I Really Want: Readings for a Modern Christmas.*

Marchaé Grair is a spiritual director and the Director of Public Relations and Outreach for the Unitarian Universalist Association.

Matt Laney is a United Church of Christ minister and the author of *Pride Wars*, a fantasy series for young readers.

Mary Luti is a long-time seminary educator and the author of *Teresa of Avila's Way* and numerous articles on the practice of the Christian life.

Kenneth L. Samuel is Pastor of Victory for the World Church (UCC) in Stone Mountain, Georgia. He is the author of *Solomon's Success: Four Essential Keys to Leadership.*

Donna Schaper is the author of 32 books, most recently *I Heart Frances: Letters to the Pope from an Unlikely Admirer.* She is Senior Minister at Judson Memorial Church in New York City.